LEARN TO READ

WITH IMAGES

Reading Made Easy With
MY FRIEND & ME

By Barnaby Pollock

This is a work of fiction. Names, characters, places, and incidents either are the product of the author's imagination or are used fictitiously. Any resemblance to actual persons, living or dead, events, or locales is entirely coincidental.

First paperback edition December 2022

ISBN 9798370015403 (Paperback)

LearnWithImages@Outlook.com

Bath time

Bath time

Pg 2   I love to play in the mud. I throw it here and there.

Pg 3   My grandma says, "Bath time now, let's go wash your hair."

Pg 4   "Where are you going? The bath is this way."

Pg 5   My good friend in the woods can give me my bath today.

Pg 6   Wash my body, wash my hair, wash between my toes.

Pg 7   Dry the water, all clean now. I smell sweet like a rose.

Pg 8   My grandma says, "You good, good boy with beautiful, beautiful clean hair."

Pg 9   I'll keep my secret in the woods, so I can go back there.

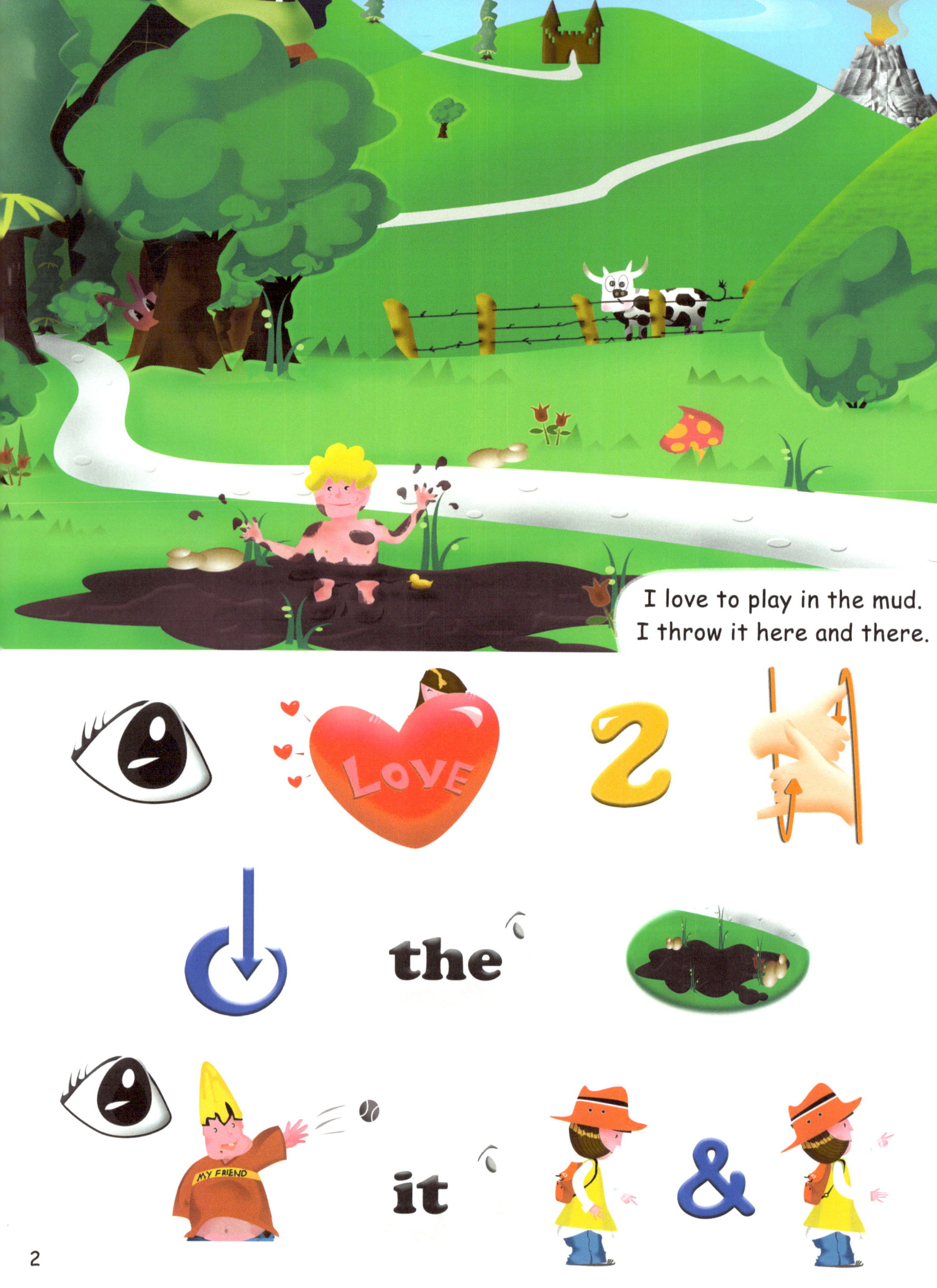

I love to play in the mud.
I throw it here and there.
LOVE
2
the
MY FRIEND
it
&

My grandma says,
"Bath time now,
let's go wash your hair."
says
Time
MY FRIEND
ME

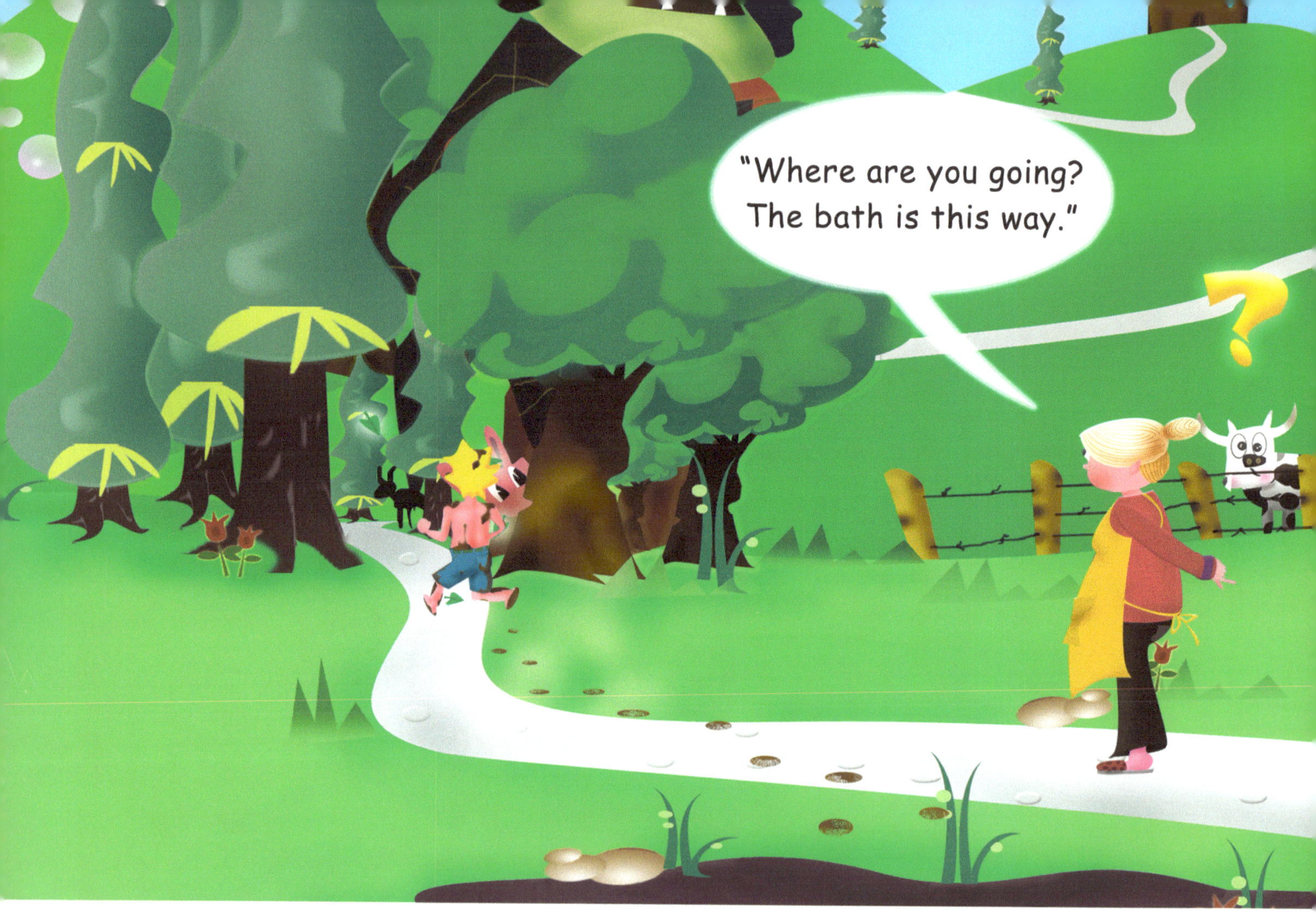
"Where are you going?
The bath is this way."

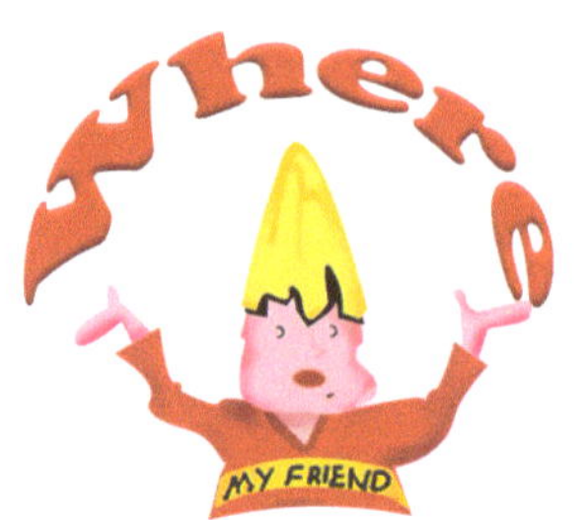

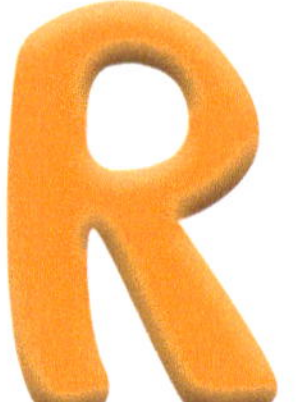

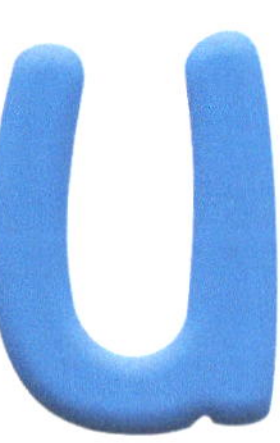

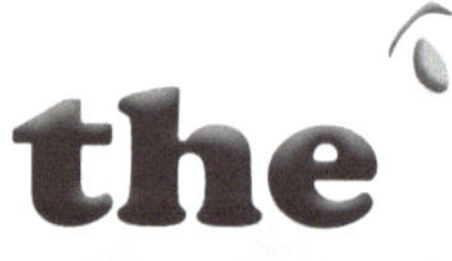

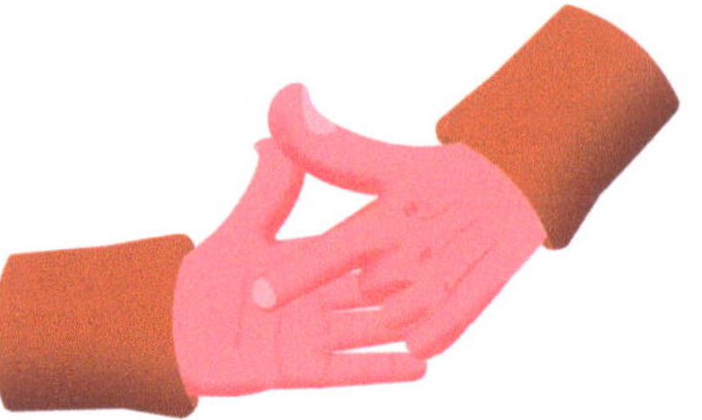

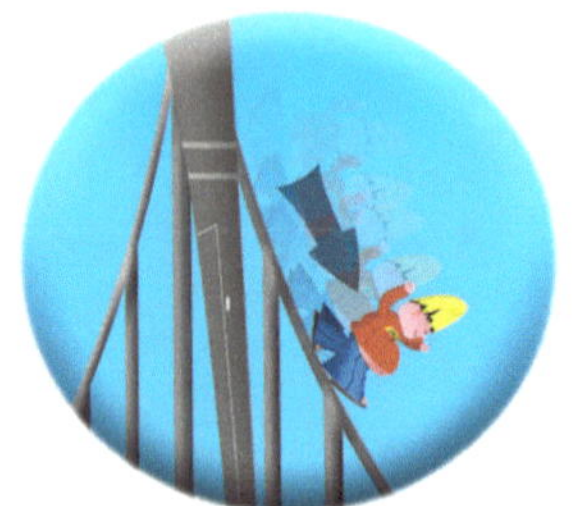

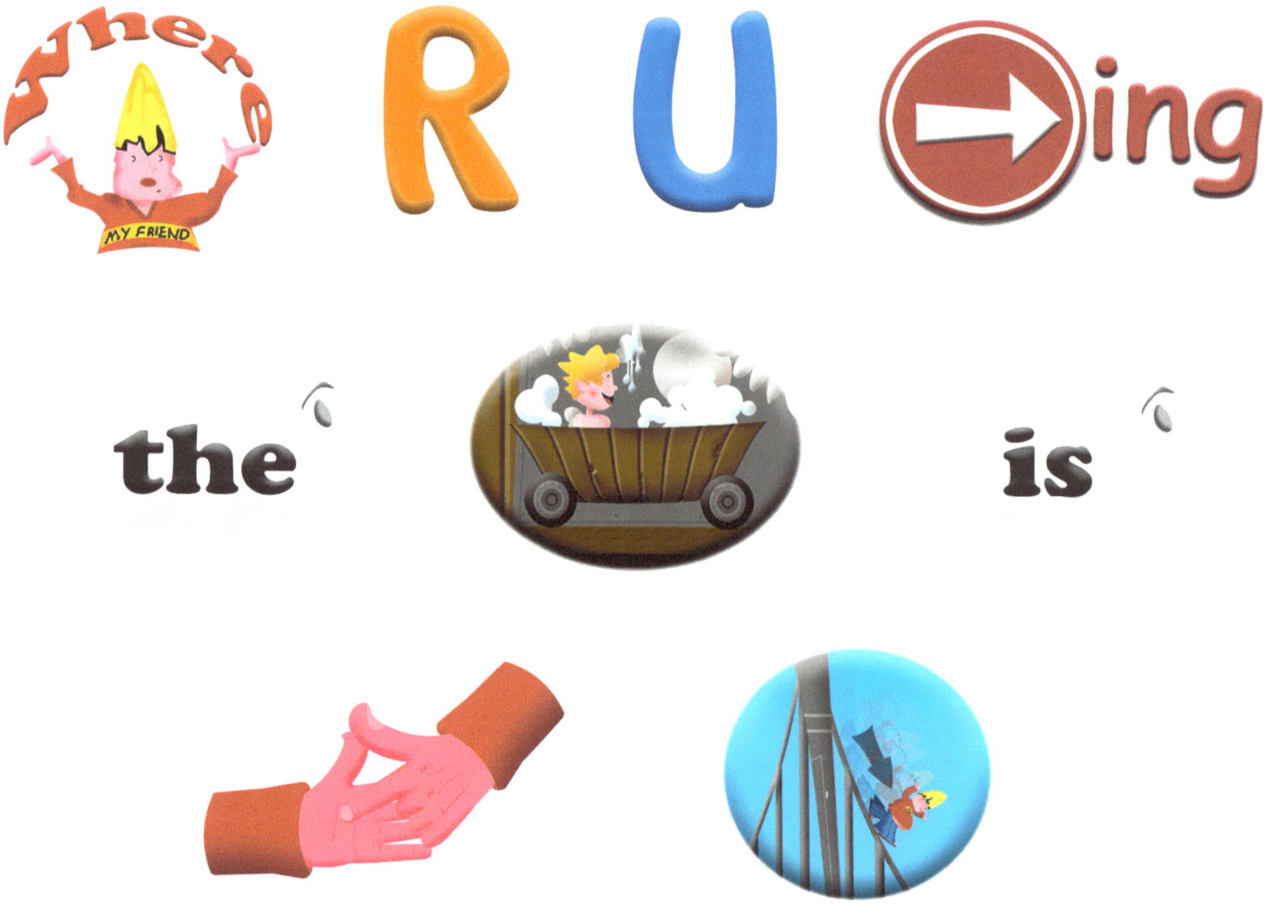
where
MY FRIEND
R U
ing
the
is

BATH TIME IN THE WOODS
My good friend in the woods can give me my bath today.
MY FRIEND
ME
the
can
ME
2day

Wash my body, wash my hair,
wash between my toes.

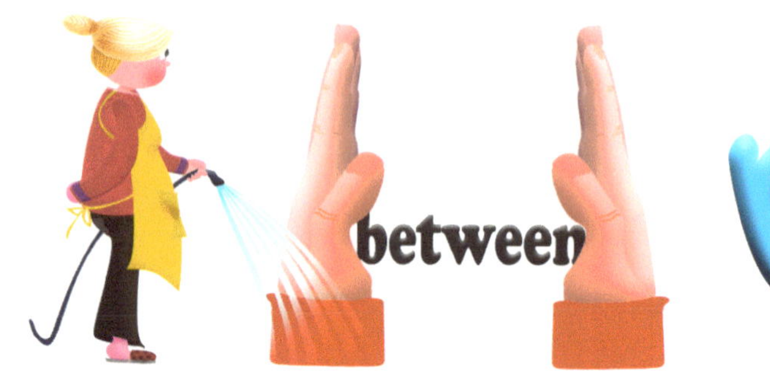

between

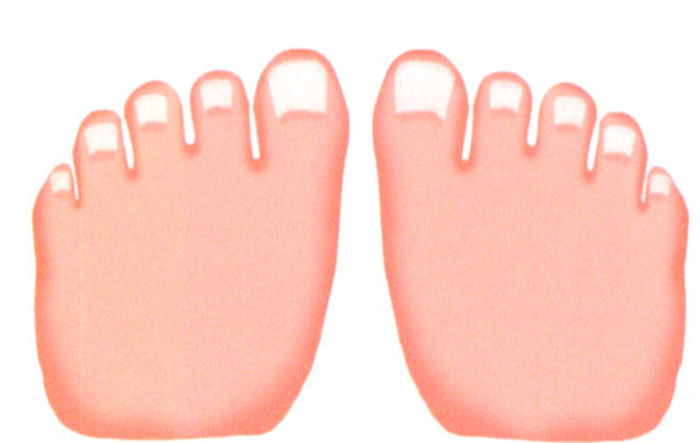

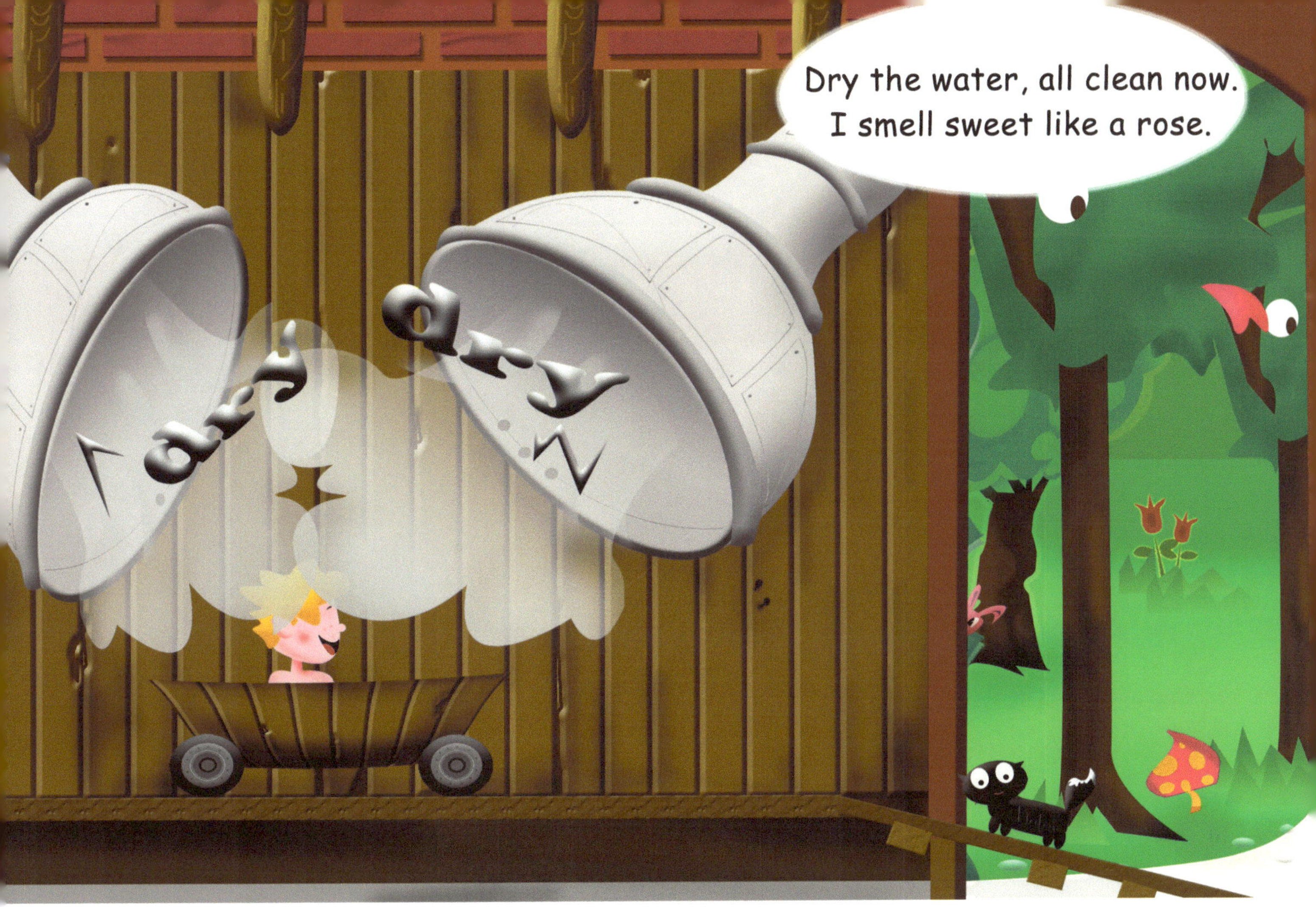

Dry the water, all clean now.
I smell sweet like a rose.

  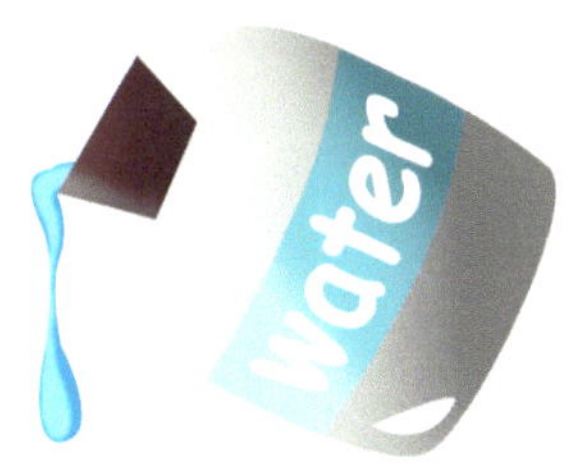

dry
the
water

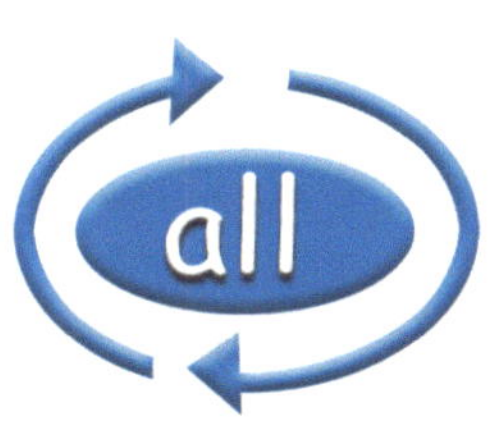  

all
clean
MY FRIEND

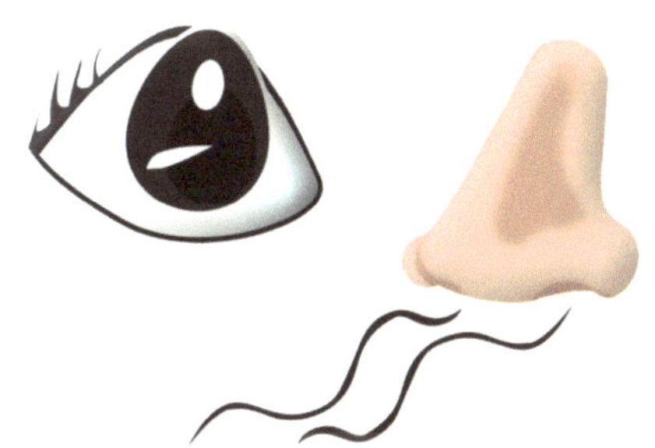    

sweet
like
A

My grandma says,
"You good, good boy with
beautiful, beautiful clean hair."
says
with
B-U-T ful
B-U-T ful
clean

9

On the way

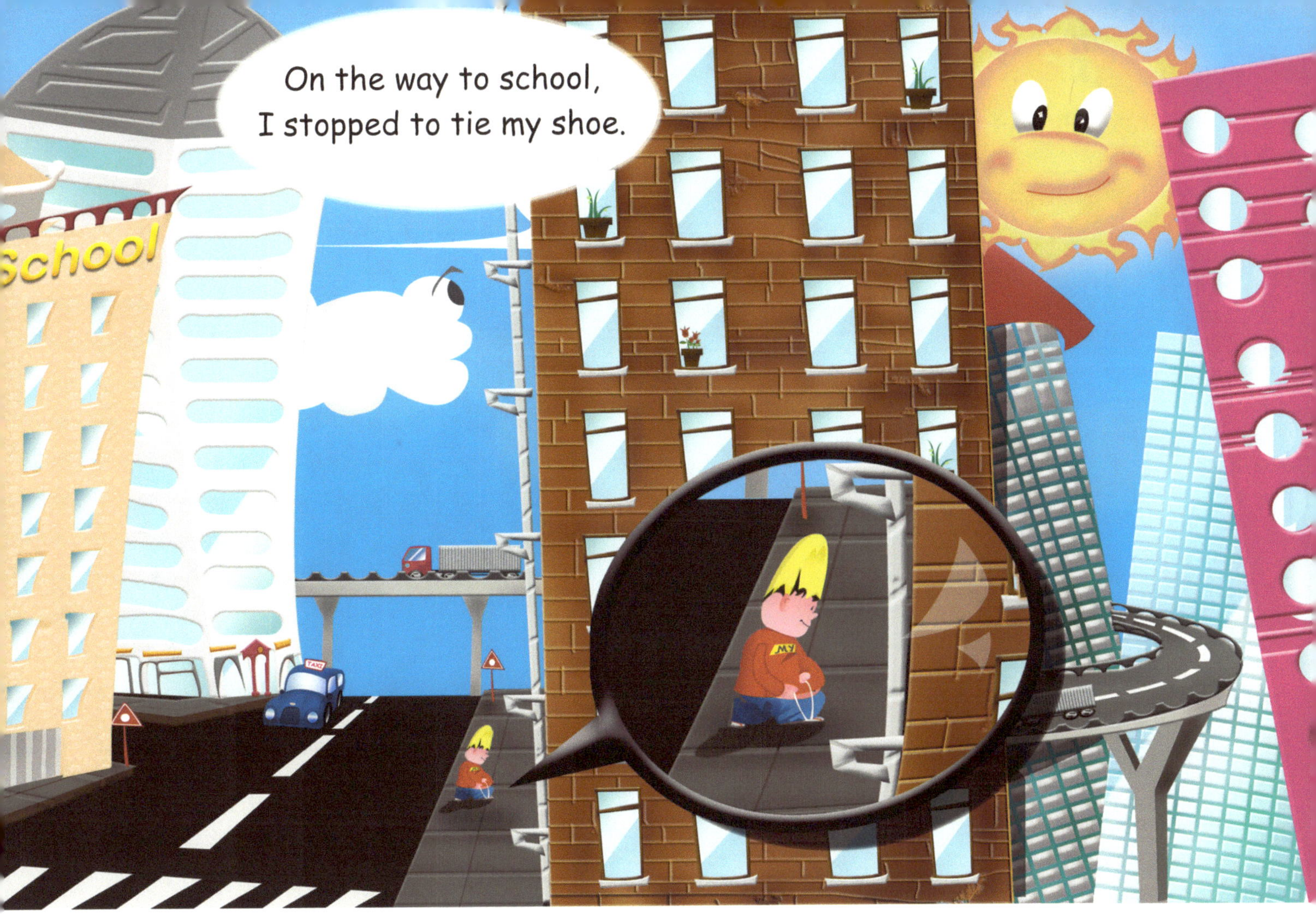

the

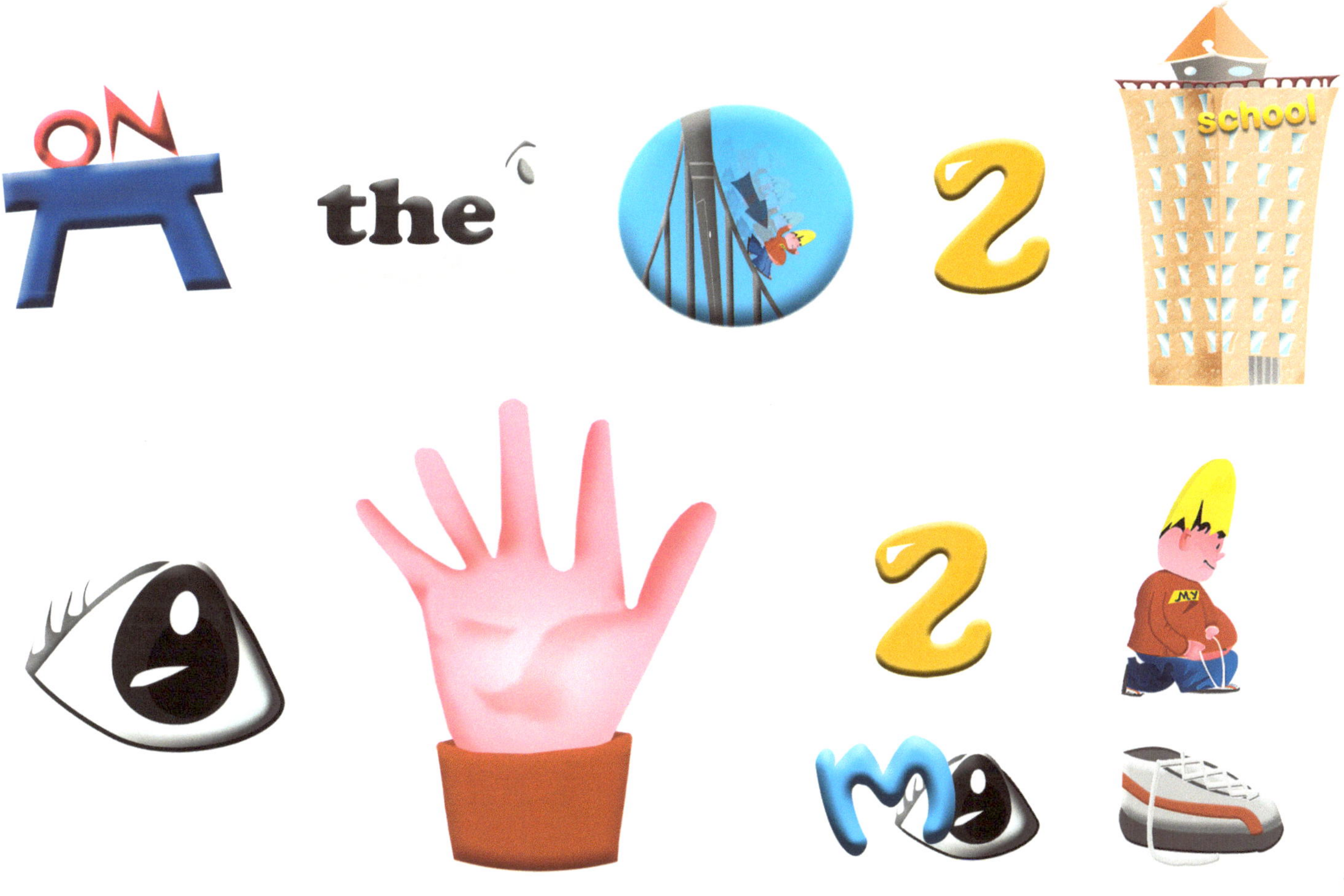

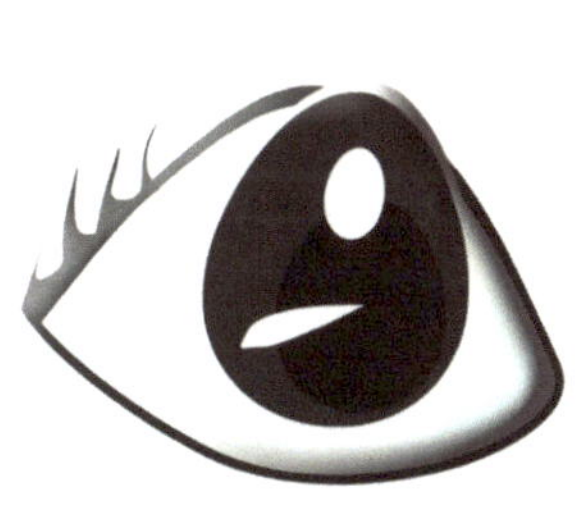

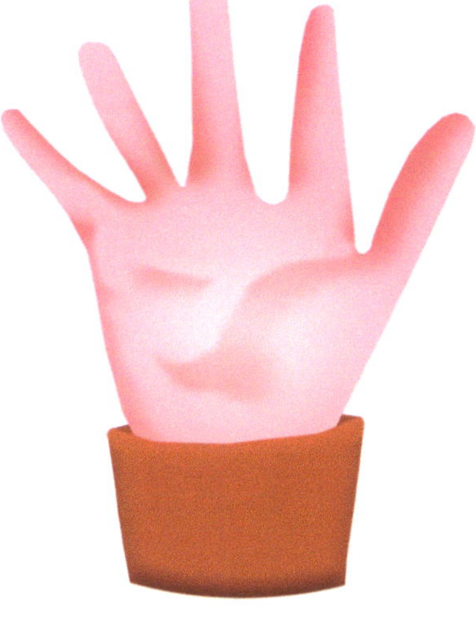

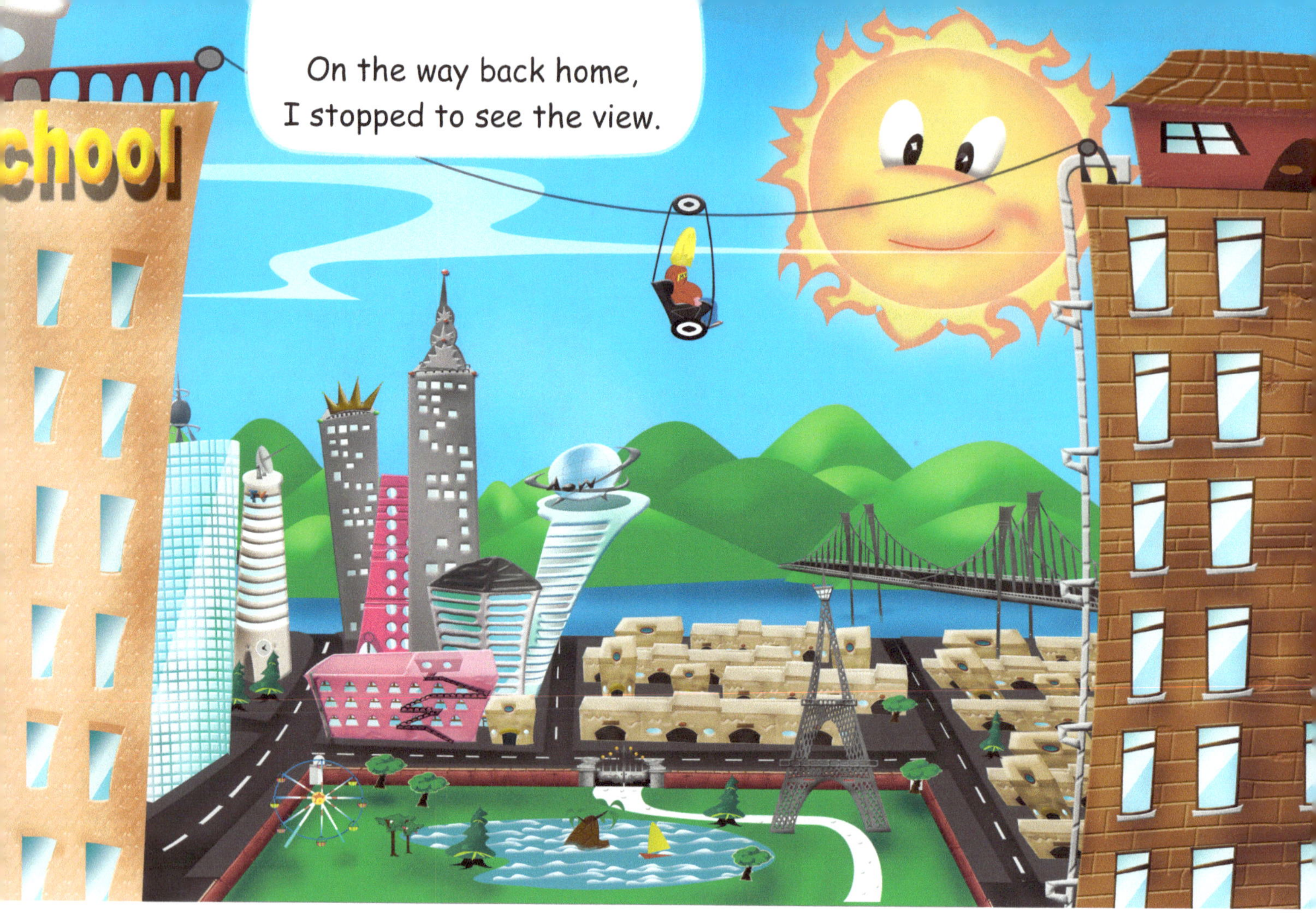

on  the   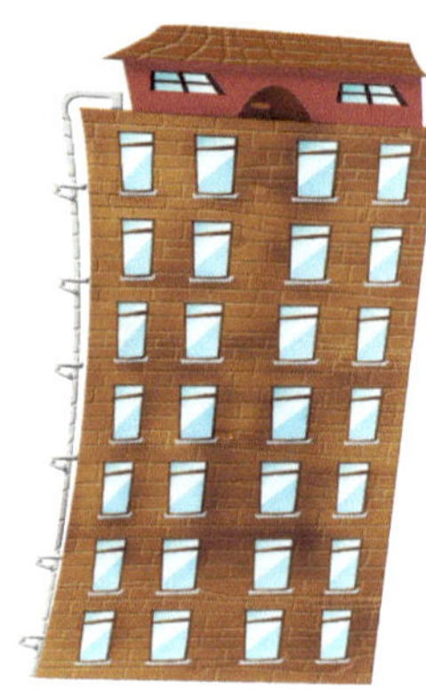

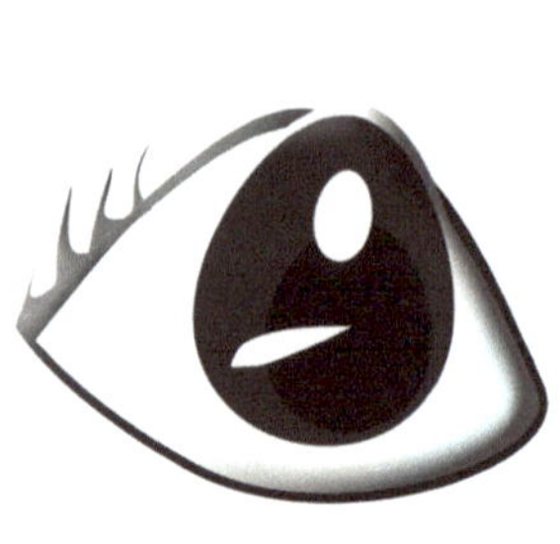 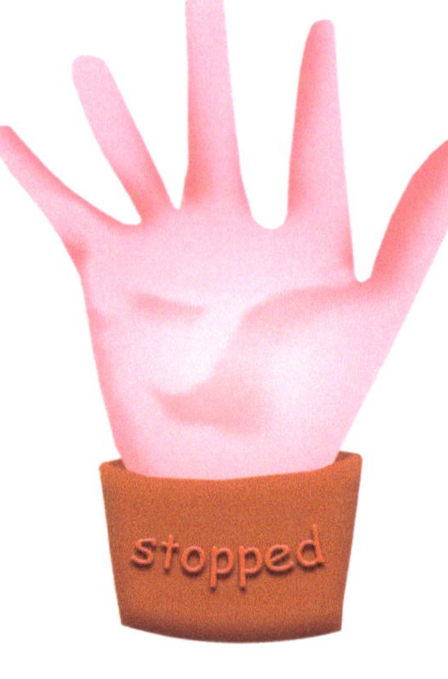

2   the 

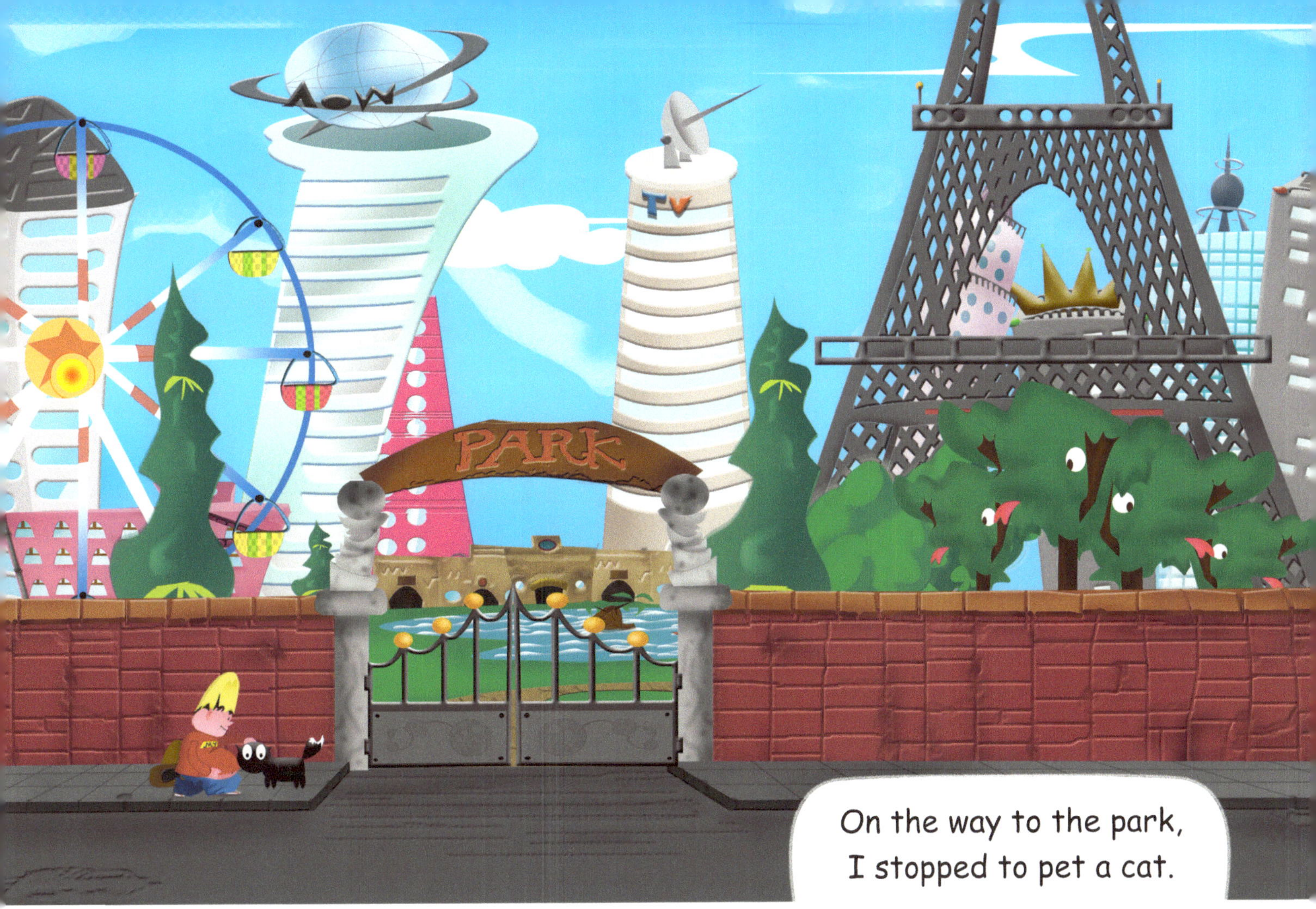
PARK
TV
On the way to the park,
I stopped to pet a cat.

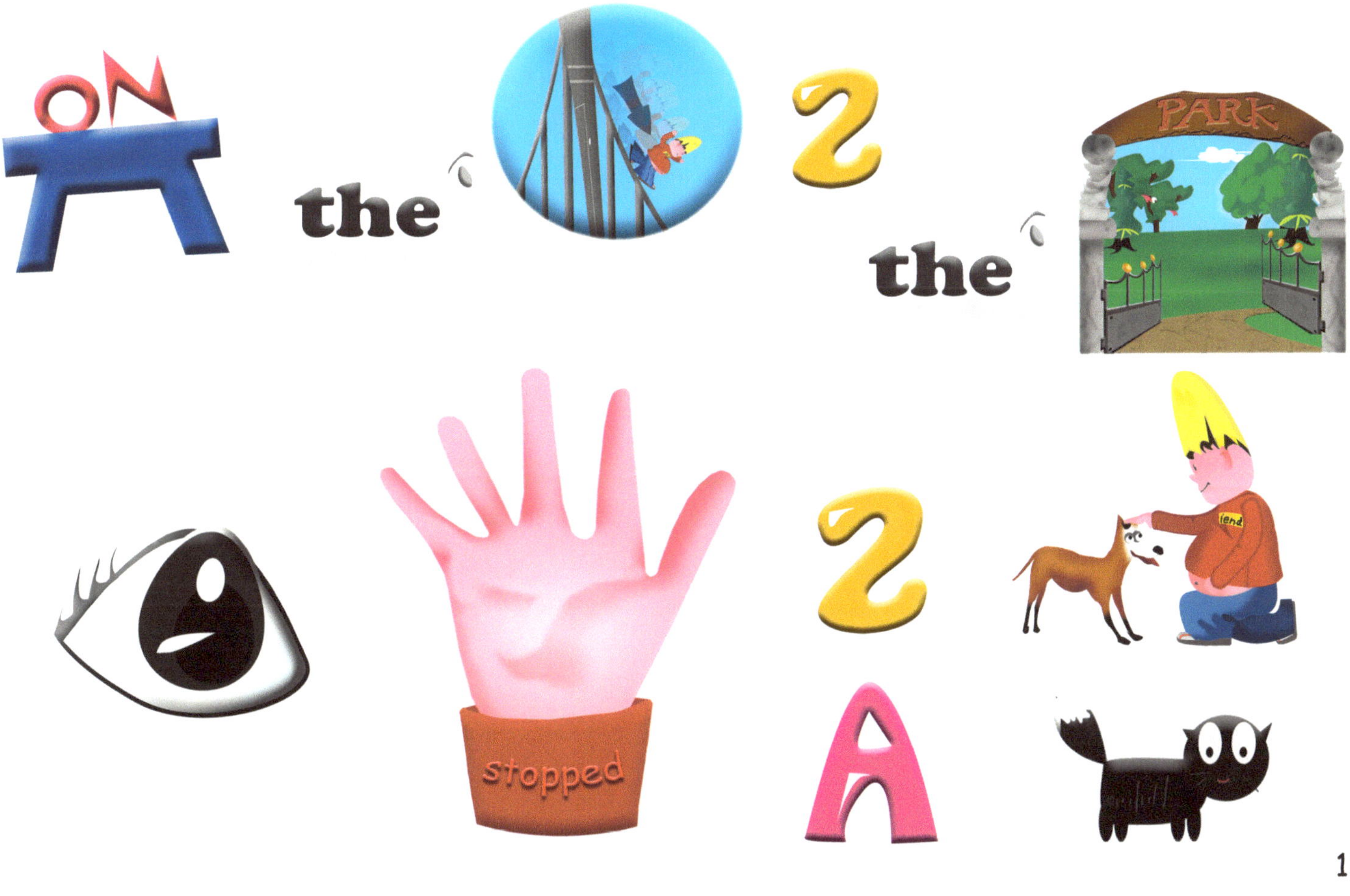
ON
the
2
PARK
the
stopped
2
A

On the way back home,
the wind blew off my hat.

On the way to see my friend,
I stopped to take a rest.

On the way back home,
I thought this way is best.

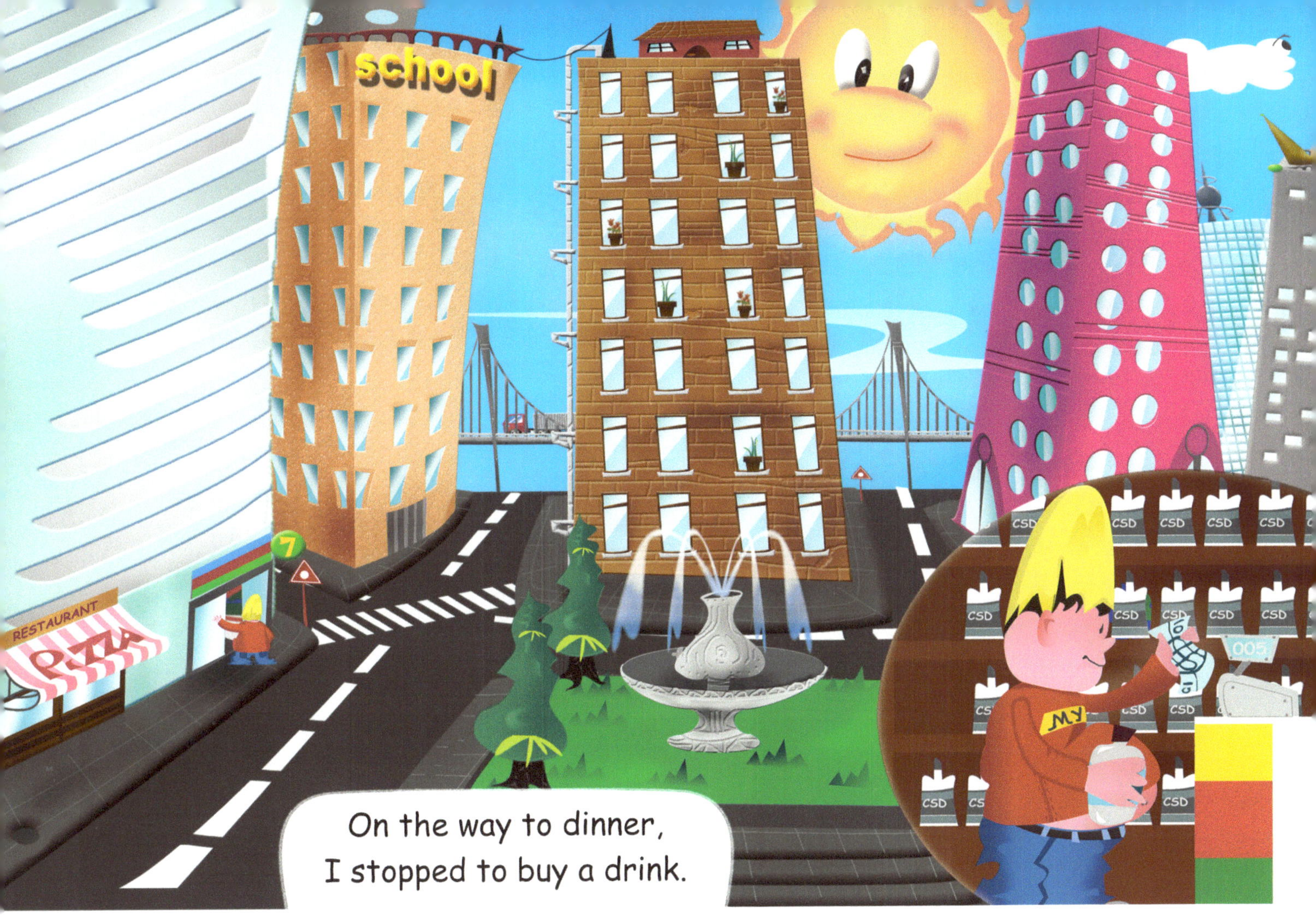

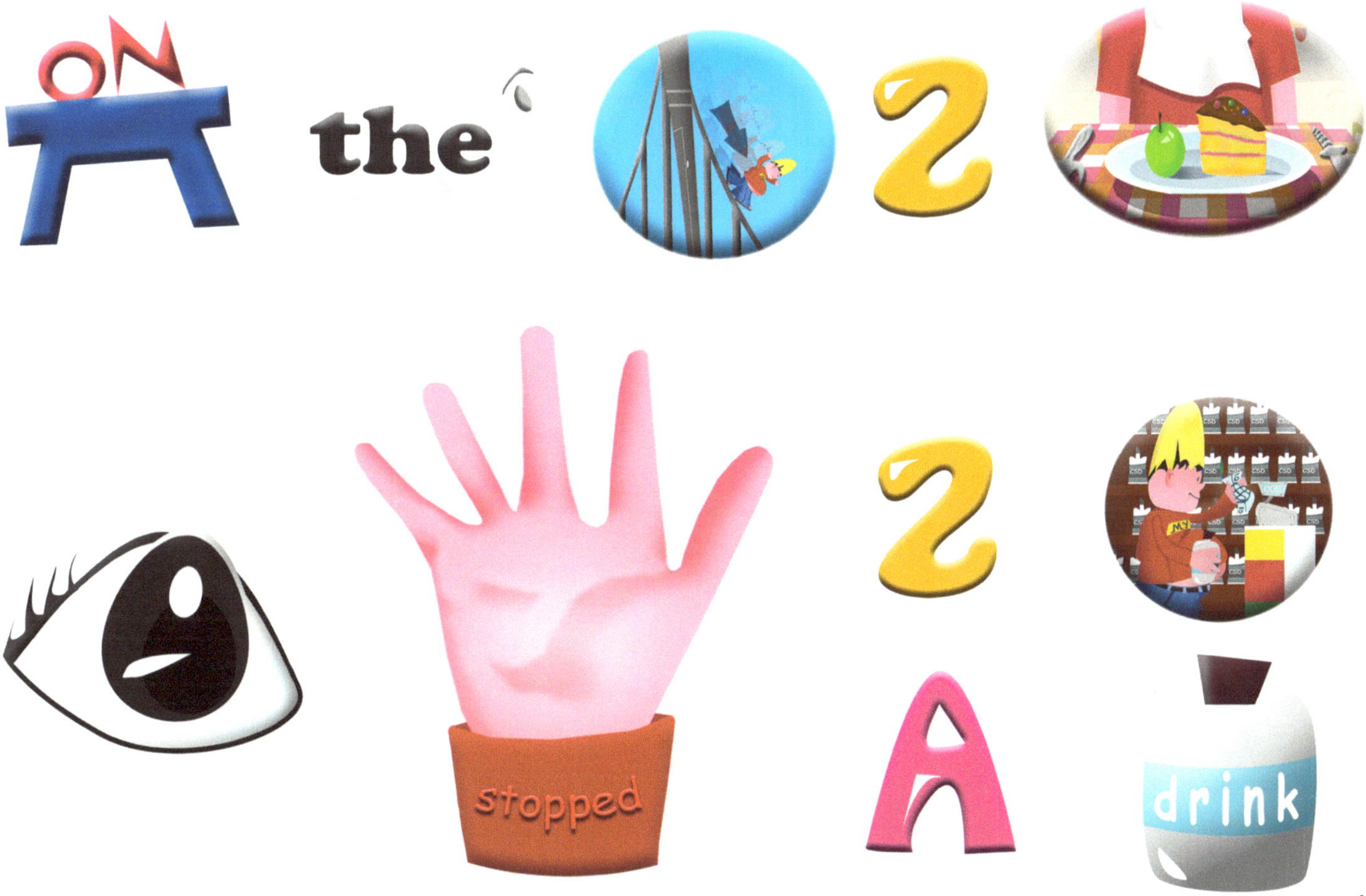

 the   

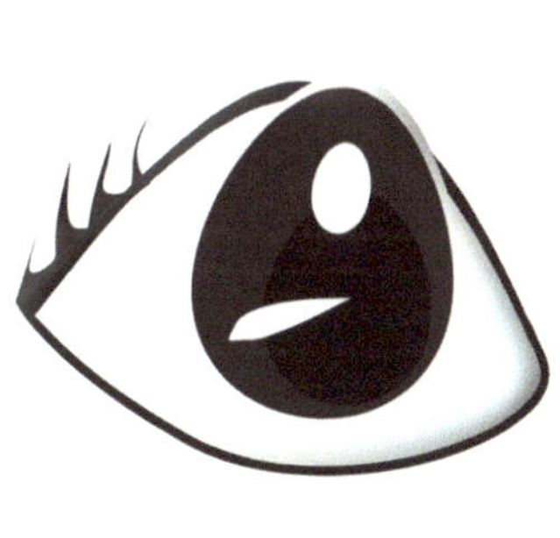 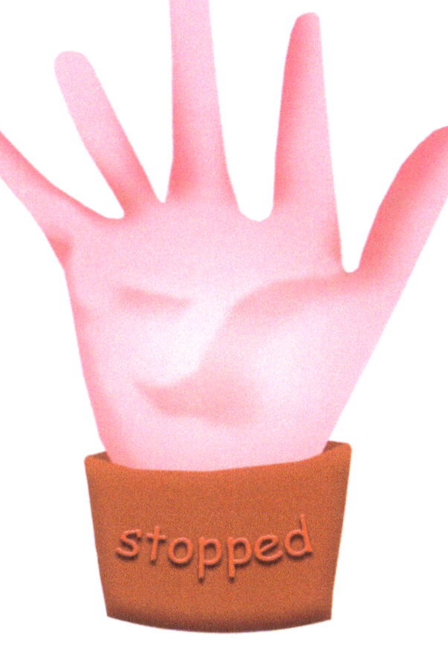  

On the way back home,
I fell asleep I think.

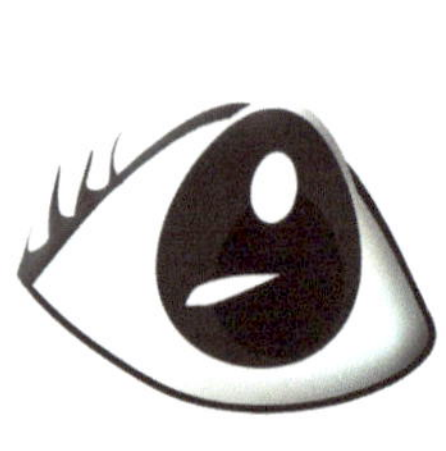

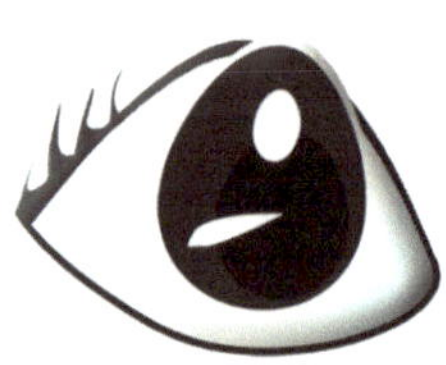

My best friend

My best friend

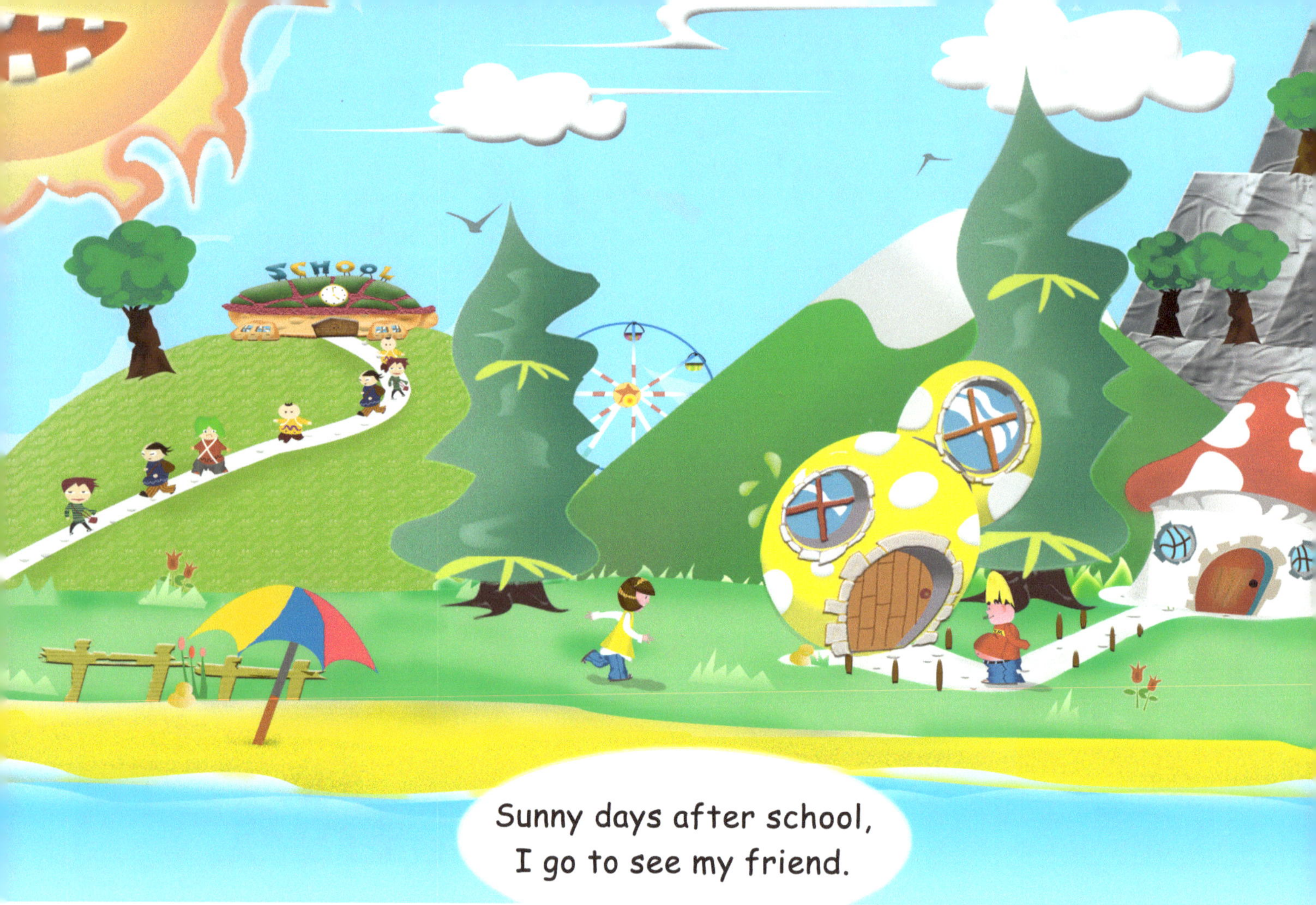
SCHOOL
Sunny days after school,
I go to see my friend.

day
S

after

SCHOOL

MY FRIEND

MY FRIEND

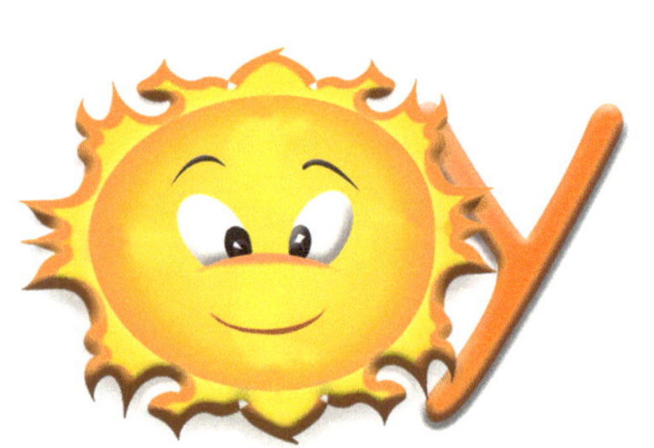

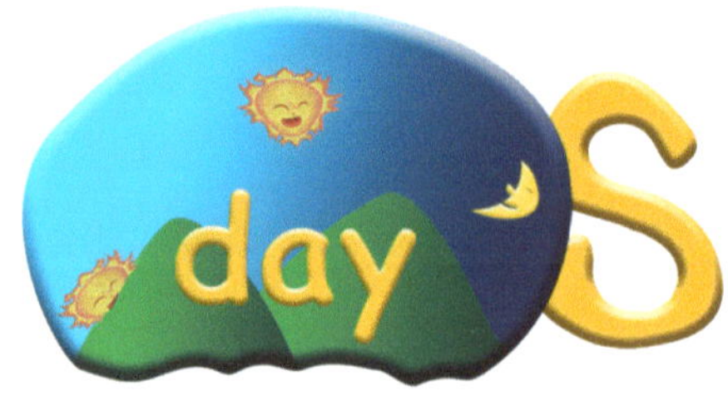

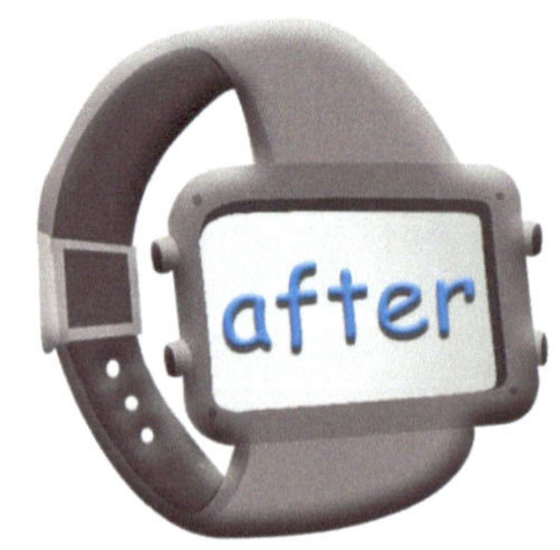

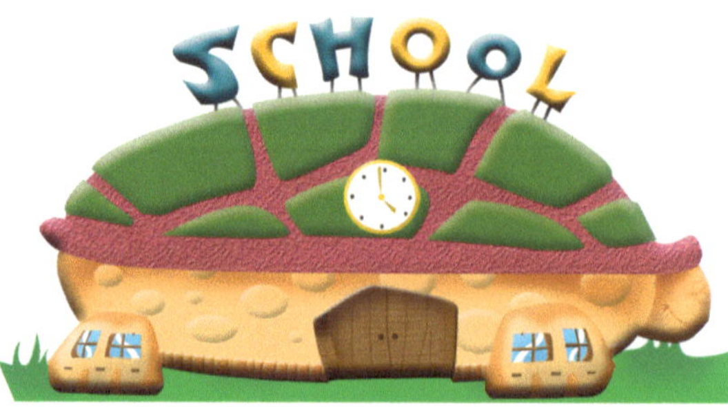

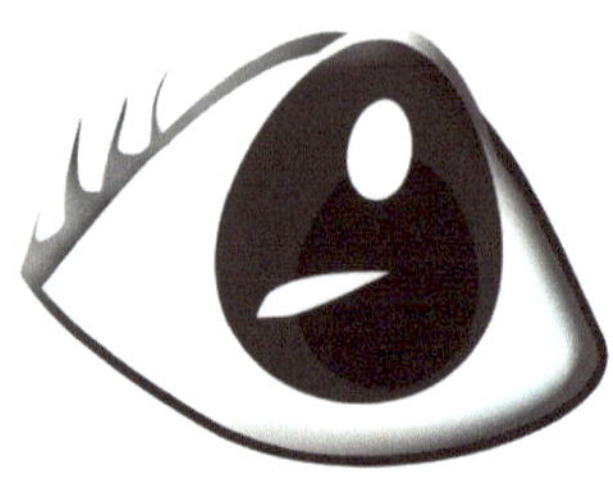

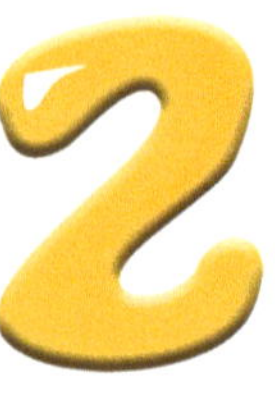

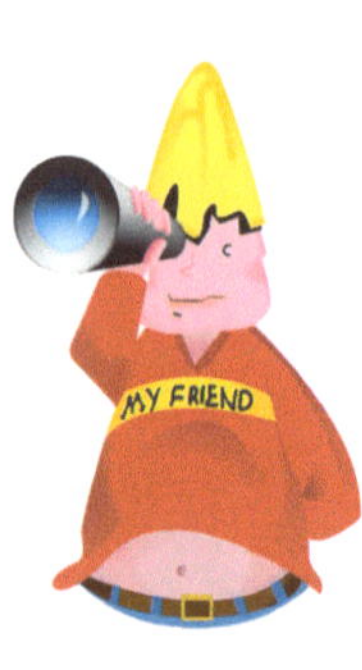

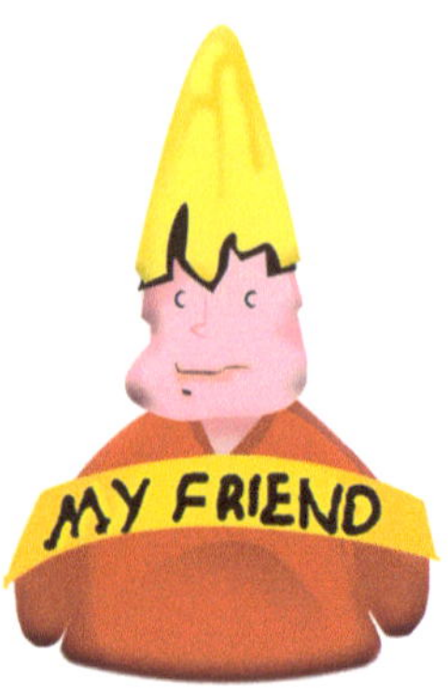

very

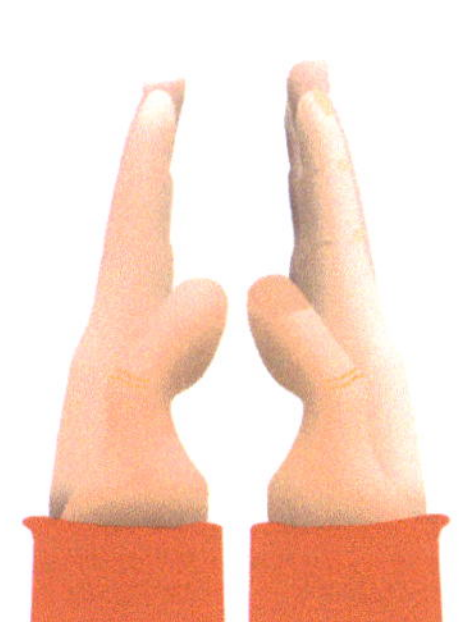

just  the 

When I get to his house
I just have to say.
When
get
2
his
just
have
2
say

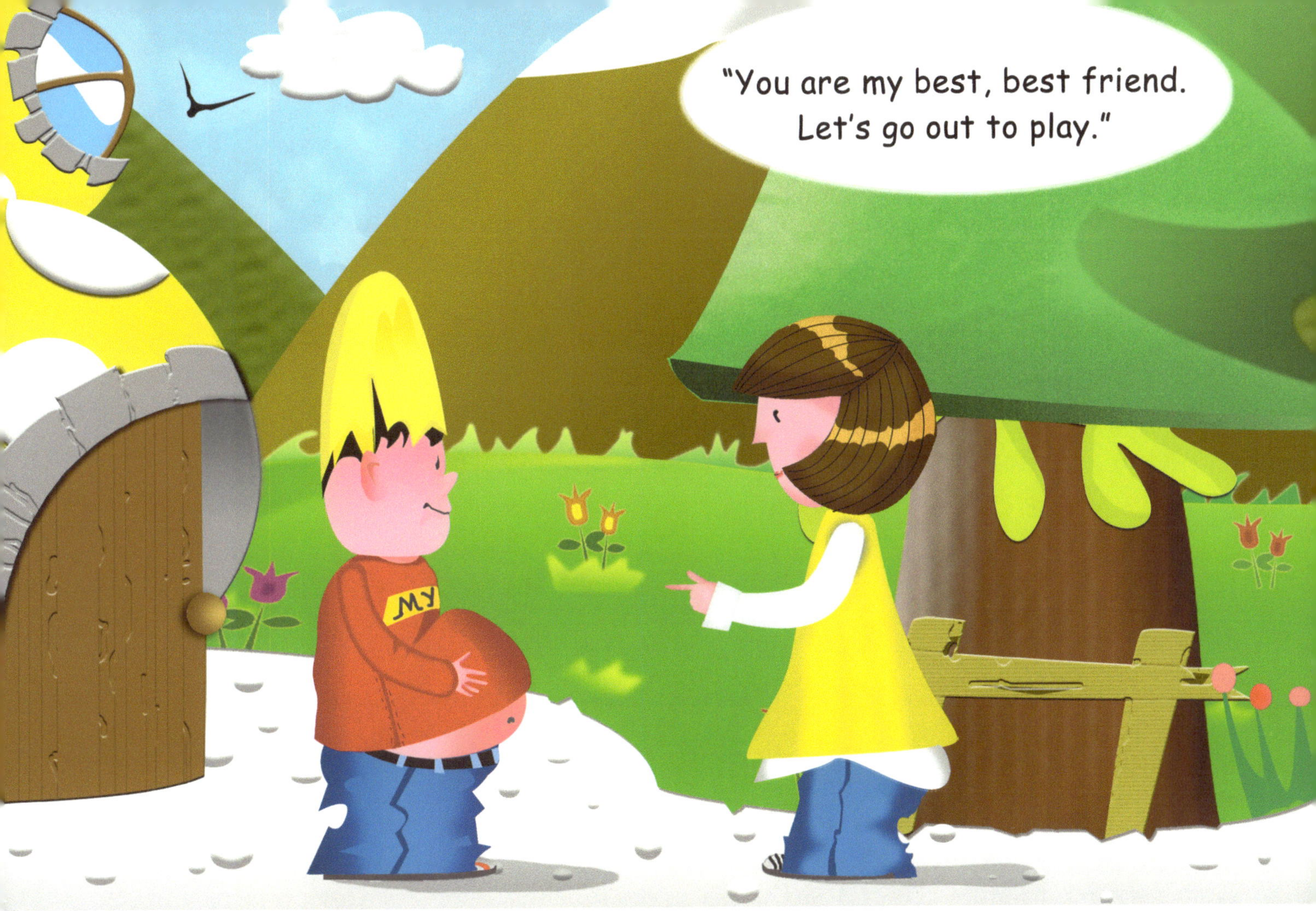

"You are my best, best friend.
Let's go out to play."

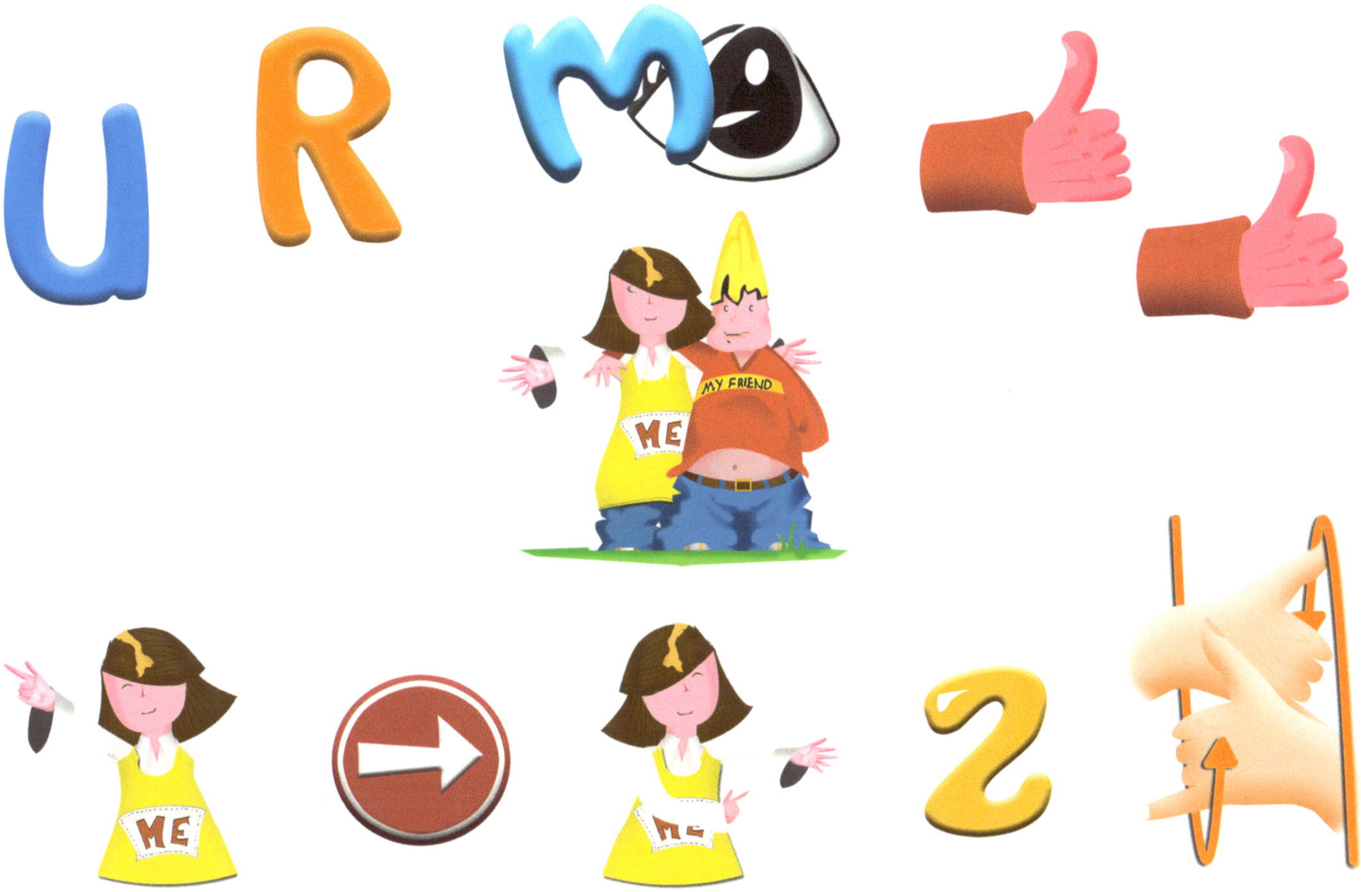

PARK
We like going to the park
and sliding down the slide.

WE

like

ing

2 the 

 &

ing

 the 

Finding all the secret places
we can go to hide.
PARK
SCHOOL

ing

all

the

ME
secret

ME
W   E

can

2

When the sun starts to set,
I go back to my house.
When
the
start
my

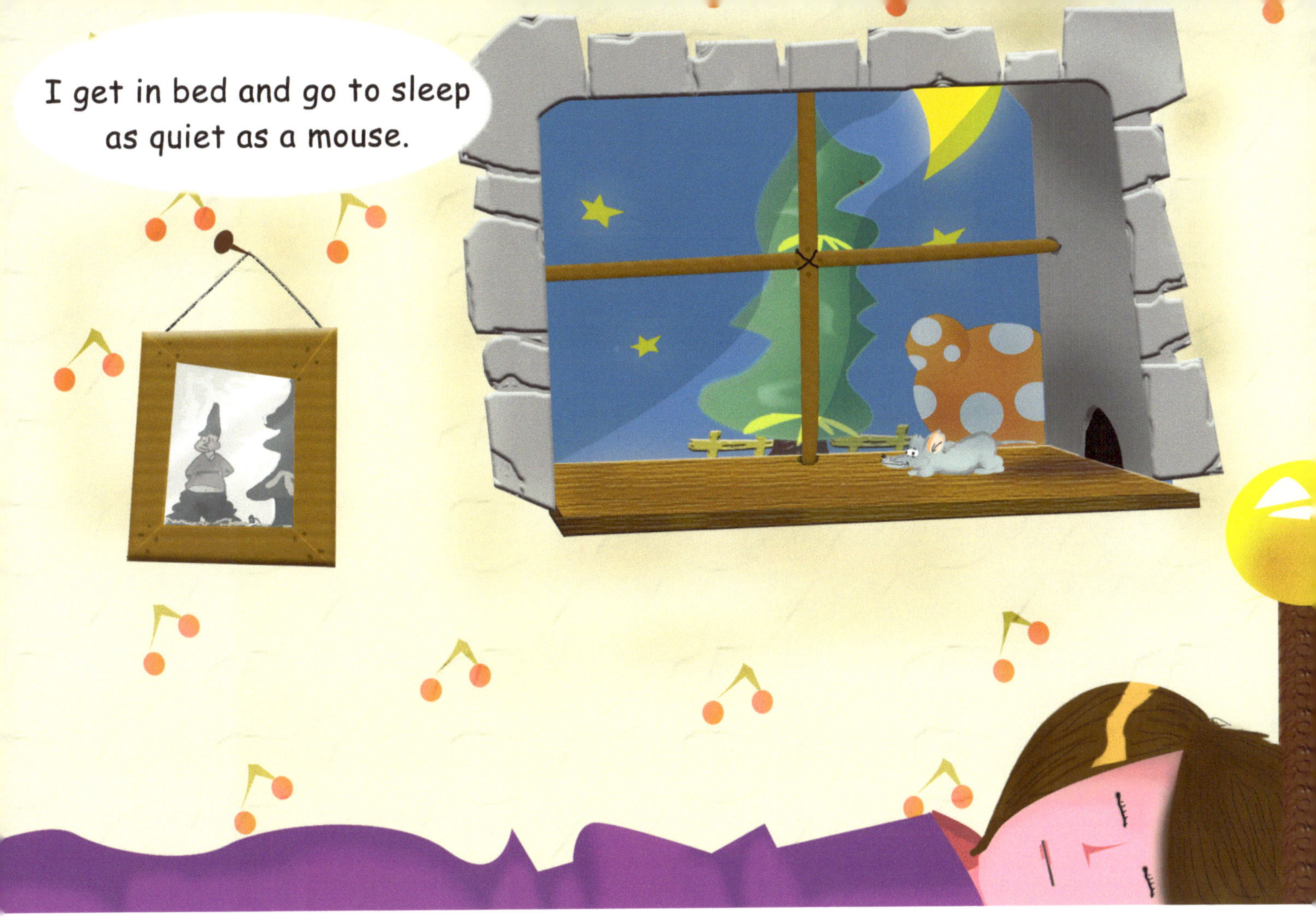

I get in bed and go to sleep
as quiet as a mouse.

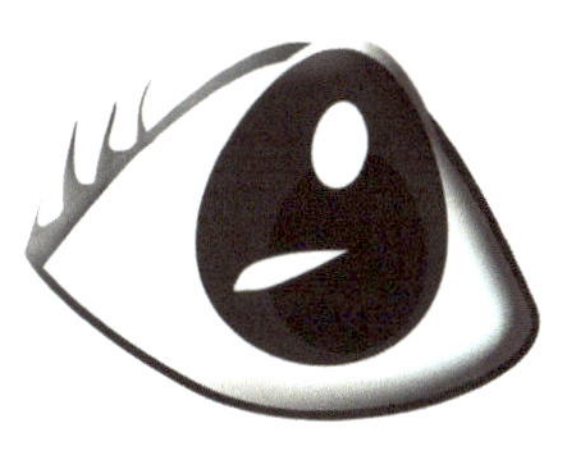  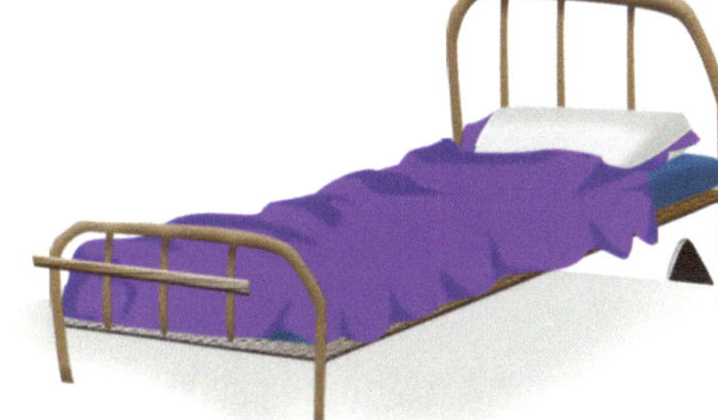

I want to be

I want to be a movie star,
so I can drive the fastest car.

HollyHood
STUDIO
recording
caution

want 2 B A
so can
the est

I want to be a park ranger,
so I can keep you from danger.
want
PARK
so
can
ME
2
B
A
U
from

I want to be the best DJ,
so I can listen to music all day.
music land
want 2 B the DJ 
so can
2 all day

Learn to Read with Imaaes
I want to be an acrobat,
so I can fly above the mat.
want
2
B
AN
so
can
the

32

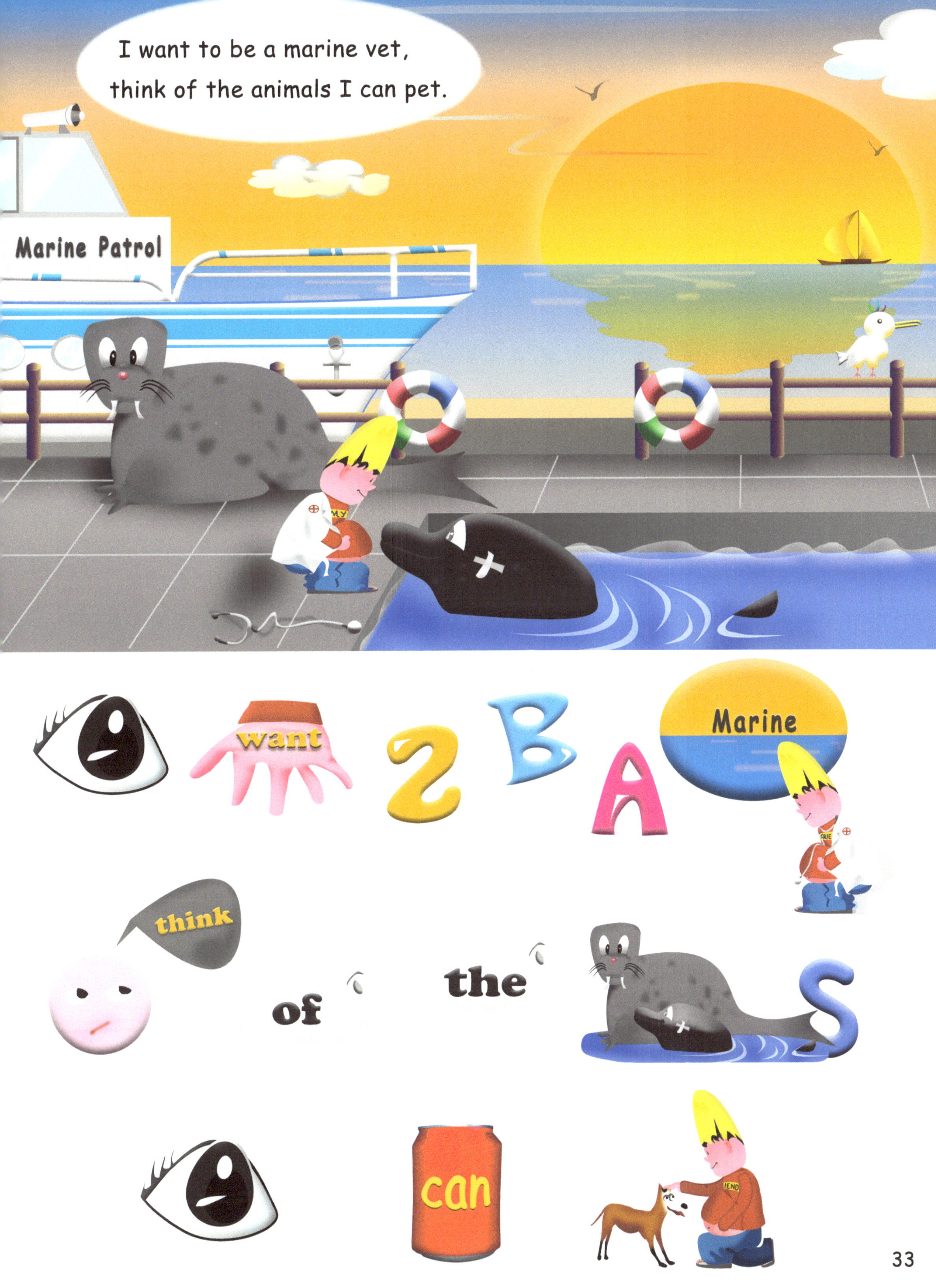

I want to be a marine vet,
think of the animals I can pet.
Marine Patrol
want
2
B
A
Marine
think
of
the
S
can

34

I want to be an athlete,
so in the Olympics
I can compete.
higher · faster · stronger.

want
2
B
AN
so
the
S
can

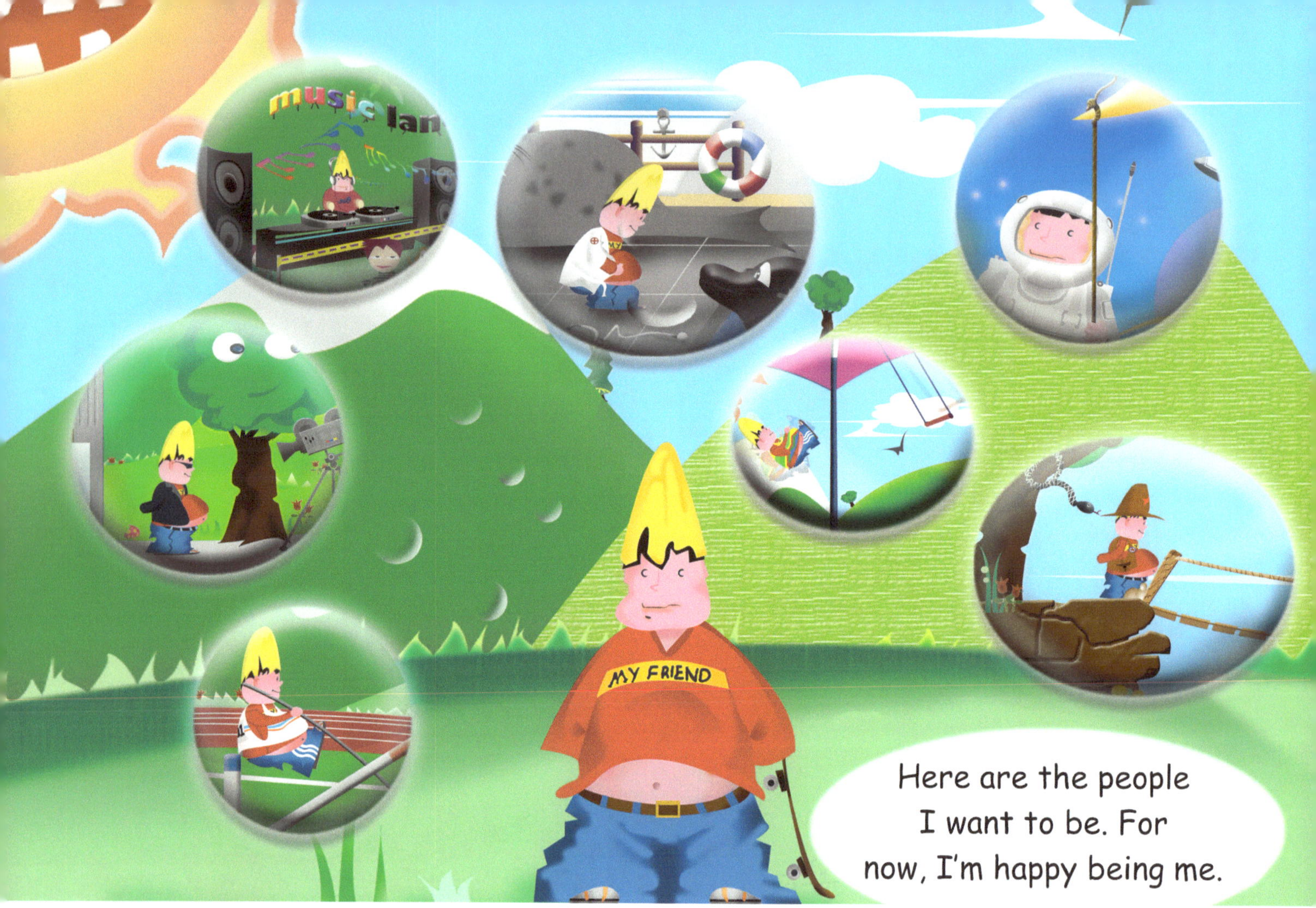

Here are the people I want to be. For now, I'm happy being me.

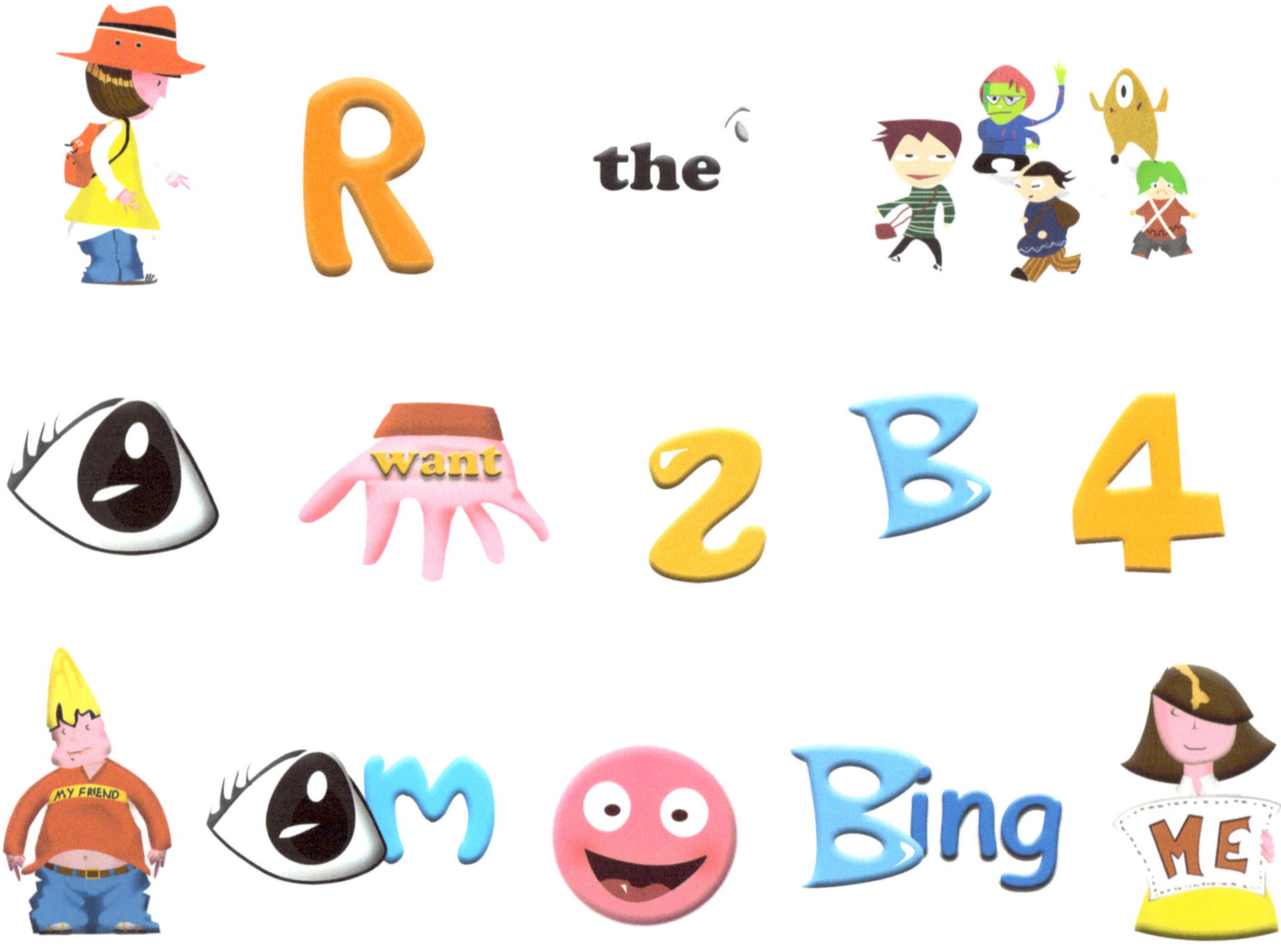

 R  the  

  want  2 B 4  

  M  Bing  

Vocabulary

A	a	(art)		marine	(adj)
	above	(prep)		me	(pers pron)
	acrobat	(n)		moon	(n)
	after	(adv)		movie	(n)
	all	(adj)		music	(n)
	and	(conj)		mouse	(n)
	animal	(n)		my	(poss)
	are	(v)	N	now	(adv)
	around	(adv)	O	off	(adv part)
	as...as	(adv)		Olympics	(n)
	asleep	(adj)		on	(adv part)
	astronaut	(n)		out	(adv part)
	athlete	(n)	P)	park	(n)
B	back	(adv part)		pet	(v)
	beautiful	(adj)		people	(n)
	bed	(n)		place	(n)
	bend	(n)		play	(v)
	best	(adj)	Q	quiet	(adj)
	blew	(v)	R	ranger	(n)
	boy	(n)		rest	(n)
	but	(conj)	S	say	(v)
	buy	(v)		school	(n)
C	can	(modal v)		see	(v)
	car	(n)		secret	(adj)
	cat	(n)		set	(v)
	close	(adj)		shoe	(n)
	compete	(v)		sleep	(v)
D	day	(n)		slide	(n)
	down	(adv part)		star	(n)
	dinner	(n)		start	(v)
	DJ	(n)		so	(adv)
	drink	(n)		some	(adj)
F	fastest	(adj)		sun	(n)
	fell	(v)		sunny	(adj)
	find	(v)		stopped	(v)
	fly	(v)	T	take	(v)
	for	(conj)		the	(def art)
	friend	(n)		think	(v)
G	go	(v)		this	(pron)
	get	(v)		thought	(v)
H	happy	(adj)		those	(n)
	hat	(n)		tie	(v)
	he	(pers pron)		to	(adv part)
	hide	(v)	V	vet	(n)
	home	(n)		view	(n)
	house	(n)		very	(adv)
I)	I	(pers pron)	W	want	(v)
	is	(v)		wash	(v)
J	just	(adv)		way	(n)
L)	live	(v)		we	(pers pron)
M	machine	(n)		what	(adv)
	marvelous	(adj)		when	(conj)
	mat	(n)		wind	(n)

On The Way Song

On The Way Song

On The Way Song

My Best Friend Song

My Best Friend Song

My Best Friend Song

I Want To Be Song

I Want To Be Song

Learn to Read with Images: An Introduction

Learn to Read with Images is a creative educational resource designed to make reading easier and more visually engaging. The philosophy is simple, effective, and suitable for learners of any age. This self-paced learning and teaching tool is highly convenient for use at home or in the classroom. It is targeted at beginner readers and is also beneficial to ESL and visual learners who struggle with literacy and breaking down phonics patterns.

Progressive Reading Levels

Learn to Read with Images is the key to unlocking each child's reading potential. There are six levels, each containing four stories that progressively increase in difficulty. Each level uses rhyme, sentence patterns, and elements of compound learning. The colorful, age-appropriate 'learning images' help early readers 'see' the words so they can connect the image to a word, and then easily decode (sound them out). By engaging more deeply with the content, readers can make quick connections, which aid significantly with vocabulary retention and memorization.

How Does *Learn to Read with Images* Work?

Learn to Read with Images is a simple, two-part learning process, as shown below.

- The upper half of each page tells a story and provides a visual environment for children to use their imagination.
- The bottom half of each page uses 'learning images' to represent the words in the story and helps with the pronunciation of more complex words.

Sight words that appear frequently are represented as 'text on a cloud' to help the students memorize words when it's time to read without the aid of the 'learning images.' This creative approach helps keep children interested so they can concentrate on learning vocabulary and fluency.

How Can You Use *Learn to Read with Images*?
It's as easy as 1-2-3!

1) As with any story, begin by reading to children, using the illustrations to help tell the story and spark their imagination.

2) Point to the 'learning images' as you pronounce each word. It is important that children learn to point to the words too, so urge them to point along with you as soon as possible. Help cement their recognition of the 'learning images' by repeatedly asking what it says.

3) Take time between pages to develop recognition of the 'learning images' by asking children to point at particular words and pronounce them. While they are not yet reading the written word, this is the first step in learning to read, which is exciting for everyone!

How Can Readers Build Confidence?

Begin with an easy 'learning image', like an eye. Keep in mind that 'learning images' are a visual tool to help make a connection between the image, its pronunciation, and the written form of the word. For example, the image of an eye is used to phonetically represent the word 'I', as well as 'eye', the actual word itself.

These regular prompts are important to ensure that children are learning to recognize the 'learning images' and not just memorizing words or sentences.

How Do You Know Readers Are Ready for the Next Level of *Learn to Read with Images*?

Once readers can correctly identify a word and its connection to the 'learning image', they are ready for the next level of *Learn to Read with Images*. There are several sight words in the text. For younger children, it is recommended to count the number of words in the text (upper half of the page) and do the same for the 'learning images' (bottom half of the page). This is a useful prompt to remind children that not all words in the text are connected to a 'learning image', and therefore, they must read from memory. As children move up the levels, they will recognize and strengthen their recognition of words, making them more fluent readers.